Table Scraps

Table Scraps

David Shumate

ISBN: 0989884600
ISBN 13: 9780989884600
Library of Congress Control Number: 2015900586
David Shumate, Clinton, MS

Acknowledgments

I found myself writing poems when my heart was touched by moments in life—some full of love, some full of heartache, and some full of eternal hope. Metaphorical observations of simple things were often an easy way to express other moments.

Table Scraps contains seventy-four poems that capture some of the most difficult times for me as well as some of the most beautiful ones. I hope whoever reads this book will find a poem that can bring a smile, bring a tear, or at least remind them that love is to be cherished every day.

To my daughters, Tara and Kelsey—you inspired me throughout my life and taught me the true meaning of love.

I'd like to acknowledge a few very dear people who encouraged me during trying times in my life: Joe Ann Ramia, Jeri Wiygul, Ruth and Kelly Cummins, Lorainne Caldwell, Jack and Jan, Uncle Jack and Aunt Gloria, and the rest of the Shumate family, Joe Bias, Greg Gearhart, and a whole lot of running friends.

Preface

When the movie bucket list came out in 2007 I was newly divorced from a marriage of twenty years. My daughters then, twelve and fourteen were living with me. I thought it would be good for me to come up with my own bucket list. As I checked things off my bucket list over the next five years, the only remaining challenge was to write this book. I had written poems all of my life and had intended on writing the book in 2007, and when that passed my goal was to write it by 2011. I continued to write poems, but I stayed too busy running and raising daughters.

I am an avid runner that took up running in 2004 and both of my daughters ran with me through the years. Running opened my world up to new adventures and also taught me how to overcome challenges, which along with my faith is reflected in many of my poems. I competed well at the local level, winning the Mississippi Track Club Master's Division in 2009 and I've ran the Boston Marathon, New York City Marathon, and the Chicago Marathon. My daughters both ran cross country and often we spent a lot of our free time running together. In fact, running the

Boston marathon a second time and the New York City marathon were both on the bucket list.

Many of the first twenty-three poems were written during the process of my divorce. When my father was diagnosed with Alzheimer's in 1997 I wrote him, "A Dad Just like You," I took him and my mom out to eat a sandwich and read the poem to him. My mom began to cry and asked my dad, "Do you understand it?" He never said a word but stared at the poem. A few years later, I wrote, "Evening Moments," as his condition worsen from the disease.

Writing was therapeutic and even an escape from the current events in my life. Three poems I wrote during my separation while living in a small apartment with the Caldwell's. Mrs. Caldwell was an amazing counselor, friend, mom, and wife. She spent many hours listening to me. I wrote, "Busy Bee" in her honor.

I moved from the Caldwell's to a basement room with unbelievable gracious friends Ruth and Kelly who opened their home to me, for five months. One of the poems, "Tucking in the Mannequins," was about my pretend friends the mannequins that imaginatively lived in their garage next to my room.

And of course, I wrote many love poems. Some were inspired by people I met and others about people I knew or thought I would like to date. Sometimes I wrote about other people's situation.

The working title of the book has always been, Table Scraps. When I was growing up I would go into our kitchen each morning and find my father drinking his coffee, or "Stump Juice" as he would call it. He read his bible every morning and it would be sitting on the table as well. We had a large chain link fenced dog pen about 80 yards from the kitchen. The dogs would stare toward the large kitchen window, where my dad sat at the table, awaiting impatiently for him to come feed them. Dad said the dogs were waiting on the table scraps. I would ask, "Why don't you just feed them regular dog food?" Dad always said, "They won't eat it anymore; they want the good stuff, the table scraps!"

Contents

Heartache, Hope, and Understanding

A Place Called Home

I resolve to go there,
a place I once longed to leave,
where dreams were made
and dreams often died.
Yet a safe haven it was
from this world to hide.
And despite all the fun
and all the traditions,
all the tears and time spent wishing
that life then was sometimes different,
it is where I come from,
the mold that cast me
into what I've become.
And though this journey
of life lives on,
of the many places I have
and have not roamed,
the place I once longed to leave
forever beckons—
a place called home.

A Dad Just Like You

What you were to me,
you will always be—
a great dad in every way.
For cinnamon toast, sometimes burnt,
for playing cards and saying prayers,
for the many gardens we grew,
for teaching me how to work with my hands
and how to use your old wood lathe,
for the days we just plain blew,
I thank God for you.
Ballplayers, even presidents,
you wanted me to see.
You knew what a delight it would be.
But for each famous autograph,
for each old coin we saved,
I'd trade for another day with you.
And though our better days together
have quickly passed us by,
my quiet times alone are filled with thoughts of you.
And when I think of our great God
who makes no two dads alike,
I thank him for making me
a dad just like you.

Evening Moments

In a gray sky
where I can see for miles,
clouds seemingly stand still
along with the passing of time,
jolting faint memories
of when I was a boy,
rocking away the troubles
that trouble me no more.
A locust sings
in a nearby pine
as night calmly falls
like loose soil in the tiller's tine.
And as the song of the locust ends,
the new song of another one begins.

Dreams in a Bottle

Dreams in a bottle—
will it wash to shore,
or will it shatter on the rocks
and sink to the ocean's floor?

Forest or the Trees

Forest or the trees—
where do I find myself
if one of these I may be?
Which one of them am I
if in the forest I'm a tree?
But if a tree among the trees,
then a forest would we be.
Or am I a forest all alone
to which the wilderness I am home?
Sometimes I find myself
pondering upon this thought:
am I lost, found, or free
in the forest or the trees?

Inside Myself

When misty thoughts cloud my days,
I sit and ponder my enduring ways,
saying why to myself.
Why not change and indulge myself
in the pleasures I have not known,
in the cravings of my own?
And then it comes to me,
a daunting thought:
whomever I can live without,
myself I cannot.
So I deviate, but never diverge,
from safe quarters of moral thoughts,
holding within, not acting upon
incarcerated pleasures
that reside inside myself.

Waterfall

Beyond the point of illusion
where answers are often found,
streaming slowly like a river
finally running out of ground,
the wrath of reality reckons
like a thunderous waterfall,
descending all emotions
within the heart's wailing walls.
And when the turbulence subsides,
we calmly flow again
into a new stream of life
toward our destined end.

Fall Has Fallen on a Broken Heart

Fall has fallen on a broken heart,
and the cool breeze blows; cold each part.
In vast fields where the wheat did grow
lay dead all of life beneath the snow.
The fiddler fiddles with a bow,
pulling it fast and then it slow,
a melody of notes and then a chord.
Love strikes the heart like a sword.

Deceit

Contorted truths, inverted ways,
whispering lies, creating a maze
for one to figure, for one to see,
for one to contemplate, for one to believe.

When

When it's only a thought,
when it's only a dream,
live a little, give a little,
but do not let yourself be bought.

Hold on to hope
if it's all you have got.
Waste not your days
waiting in haste
for what you think is due you
or lies to change that remain untrue.

Hold on to hope
with what grip you can.
See that it does not slip
from the grasp of your hand.
Take charge of your change,
lead onward to what will be new,
and never give up on hope
that lives in little pieces in you.

Run the race as if it's the last.
Run the race as if to finish first.
See only yourself as afflicted,
never defeated.
Run strong throughout it all.

Listen to your heart,
but carefully survey the grounds
of where you have been
and are standing upon now.
Destinations are simply a place
where journeys end,
and yet it is the journey itself
you may often question—
not the destination,
but how you got there.

Life is shorter than you think.
Waste not a single day.
Be bold to face every tomorrow
as if the last one is today.
Sing when you can sing.
Dance when there is time.
Love when you are loved,
and continue to give when you question why.

Yours is a gift, a life ready to live.
Go it alone when you must.
You will always have a friend.
Learn to be lonely
yet at peace with yourself.
And when you have done well,
take time to rest.

Never look back
and ask, "Did I do what was right?"
Questions of the past
will haunt anyone's life.
But run in a way
that tomorrow will bring
the hope of a brighter day
along life's adventurous way.

Teach others the good you have learned.
Learn to teach from your own mistakes.
See to it that deception is not in you.
Master the good of life and then give it away.
Take time to listen
to the heart of anyone
whose heart needs to speak.
You may not understand
the road they've traveled,
but encourage them always.
When good comes together,
it strengthens us all
in all our ways.

Table Scraps

Pieces of life
left over from the past—
we throw them away
or give them to the dogs.
According to your desires,
you decide what to eat,
but what you discard
may be the better treat.
Old pieces of the past
are meaningless at times,
but those pieces of life
become a feast for you to dine.
It's not what you have
that will make you laugh,
but memories from the past—
life's table scraps.

I Paint Me

I paint me in colors I do not see,
abstract as art could ever be.
Yet together the picture blends
each stroke of the brush vividly,
from colors that loom
as if dark and light
come together in swirls
spinning day and night,
like the evolution of life
carefully covering the canvas—
a painting still wet, being painted,
one of shades and hues explaining
a life lived that is still changing,
becoming what it will be.
I paint me.

Possibilities

I look forward to the future
with all that I have experienced.
I am smarter now than I have ever been.
Pages of my past I have given to the wind
to carry to the grave their remnants' end.
I am wiser now, and though some would say
with wisdom comes patience and greater discretion—
when to speak, when to wait—

life is not meant to be lived timidly
running from the rain, afraid of getting wet,
living on things you almost did
but haven't yet.
Sweet memories linger for a while.
Regrets can be harder to forget.

No, if anything
I have learned to be bold,
looking forward to the future
and the possibilities it may hold.

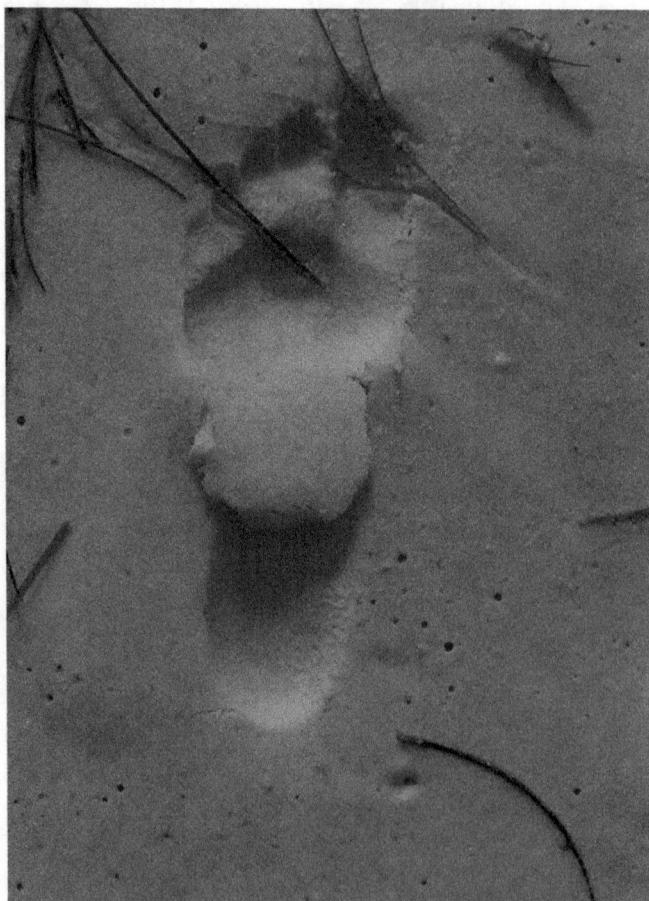

Walking by the Sea at Night

In the darkness,
I hear the whisper of the waves,
as if the sea wants to speak.
What is this ocean telling me?

So intently I listen to my soul
as the waves break
and then recede.
Is this ocean speaking to me?

I stop and listen to the waves that crash,
hoping life's answers will be found,
but the waves quickly disappear
In the sand that silences their sound.
The tranquility of the moment
reminds me that in this life;
our waves are always crashing,
and moments of quietude can only be found
if we keep our feet on solid ground.

So I walk, shuffling through the sand
as the waves of life crash to land,
and I find my peace in the little light
that guides my feet
while walking by the sea at night.

Letting Go

When an end must come and letting go is all I can do
and all the pictures I have are of you,
I'll try to remember the good times
for what they were. They were the best this life had to
offer.
It just never could have been better.
I hope we can forgive each other
for the bad times.
They were more than a few,
but the memories I have do not lie—
the best part of my life was spent with you.
I love all of life that we have shared,
and I had hoped that you would always be there.
Yet when, at the end of the day,
I think I have tried but no longer can reach you,
letting go is all I know to do.

The Night Travels By

By and by, the night travels by--
if asleep, I mean.
But relish not the current times
when everything dreamed
is in the realms of what reality seems.
Sometimes life is not good, at best.

By and by, the night travels by—
if awake, though it goes by slow,
and you alone then must face
the fickle facets of your days
that wake you in a somber way,
freezing your focus on what you crave
as you lie sleepily awake.

But everyone often garters their thoughts,
selling themselves on notions bought.
Some will sleep, and some will lie awake,
pondering the past until dead in their graves.
And some merely die
by and by, as the night travels by.

There Are Still Cookies in This World

When the winds of personal destruction have blown
and your emotions are all you own—
the unhappiness, the loneliness—
your world that has come undone,
And you believe your past
is a better path that the one you are now on,
there are still cookies in this world—
chocolate chip, peanut butter, macadamia nut,
and the list goes on and on.

Life does not always seem to have a purpose,
and some days you just don't understand,
but be assured of new paths you take and choices you
make,
you may never comprehend.
Even if you do your best, every day is not going to be a
pearl.
Yet seek peace and pleasures in the treasure of time.
There are still cookies in this world.

The Passing of Time

Mystery moves me,
yet I am not sure
what good the days are
if mystery is full of misery.
Quiet enjoyment is not offered
from the inner soul that does not sleep.
Once there was peace of mind.
Now sand does not easily fall
through the hourglass, I find.
And though the moment would suggest
time is against me,
sand still trickles
as does the passing of time.

Falling Fences

One fence falls.
One still stands.
'Tis not the cause,
always the wind.
And all we see
is the grass and sand,
and the fence that fell,
and the one that stands.

Busy Bee

I see his splendor
in the quiet moments of a busy bee,
working the delicate petals
of a Crete Myrtle feverishly.
In the still morning air
of an August day,
a gentle breeze blows
and stirs the trees,
but it does not stop
the workings of a busy bee.
It's his creation at work
in a simple bee,
yet it imitates all of life
as we work facing trials and strife.
For a bee, it's a gentle breeze.
It's something else for you and me.
Faced with toils, surely it has known.
The simple life of the busy bee goes on.
The busy bee endures and continues to give
to all of life in which it lives.
Each day it works patiently,
overcoming the trials of a busy bee.

Hope Is a Road

Hope is a road that runs between
mountains of hopelessness
and above their streams.
It will not deliver us from the mountains,
but it is a passage that leads us through.
Hope is a choice.
When we choose to change,
it is a path of uncertainty
that meanders and bends.
Hope is a road—
when traveled, it never ends.

This Little Town

This little town,
with its little brick streets
and several stoplights
are always stopping me.
Early in the morning
just before dawn,
I run past its shops
when the lights are never on.
And when this little town
finally awakens,
it rubs its sleepy little eyes
and gives its head a shakin'.
It comes alive
with all the familiar sounds
heard only here
in this little town—
the whistling of the trains,
the noisy interstate,
the places people eat,
and the places where they play,
the bustling of everyone,
the gossip that goes around,
becoming the talk
of this little town.
And though I threaten often
one day I'm going to leave,
it's not the stoplights

that are stopping me,
but the life I have found
in this little town.

The Painted Face of a Clown

Only the clown knows that when he frowns
With a painted face, he can always smile.
But with a tear, his smile will smear,
and his unpainted face reveals his cheer.

The Aftermath and Recovery

A Moment of Hope

There was a moment of hope when you came along,
like spring itself when everything's new—
such was I when I met you.
Each conversation was much more than words,
like flowers in a field under heaven's warm sun.
They bloom and dance not on their own.
Your smile, your thoughts, things in your heart—
every time we talked, I felt them all.
A moment of hope indeed you are.

Crazy Clouds

The crazy clouds that dance and fly
have no place that they must go,
yet they pretend to be everything we see,
constantly changing, endlessly.
Illusions of life caught in the sky,
like clowns, dogs, and mountains that fly,
an old man smiling with a tear in his eye,
all under the sun.
With the same winds that blow,
eventually they fall as rain or snow,
and only the sun remains in the sky
while all of life passes by.

A Poem Am I

I paint the world in black and white,
with adjectives and verbs,
bringing it to life
in a rhythm of words.
I can change day into night.
I can catch the breeze and hold it still
or let it go and send a chill.
I can bring happiness or sorrow
today or tomorrow.
I am a river of words that whisper by,
streaming together. A poem am I.

The Ocean Sleeps

The ocean sleeps by the sandy shore.
As its lazy waves tumble, the ocean snores,
and the little ghost crabs, with their tiny feet,
patrol the shore as the ocean sleeps.

Time to Rest My Soul and My Soles
(Thoughts from St. Andrew's Bay)

Staring out the window of my room,
I see boats docked in a bay—
picturesque like a jigsaw puzzle,
yet it's as real as the day.
Miles from the familiar
with many more to go,
I prop my feet in the window seat,
taking time to rest my soul and my soles.
Two black Labs play in the yard
like lovers who are best friends,
always anxious to welcome me again
with a simple licking of my hand.
The marsh's grass and pines that grow
stretch shadows across
the mirror glass
of the water's rippling rows.
If only we could love and trust each other
like faithful dogs that play,
not worrying about tomorrow's troubles
but enjoying life today.
The sun pierces through the Spanish moss
one final time, winking before it goes,
as the tranquil life I wish to live
lives outside my window.

More Beautiful than Rainbows

More beautiful than rainbows,
greater than our dreams,
are moments we choose
to love and live.
Pictures treasured most
are the memories of our hearts,
moments spent
with our families and friends.
We choose to live
without vengeful wrath,
enjoying the adventures
with people God puts in our path.
More beautiful than rainbows,
greater than our dreams,
are the moments we choose
to love and forgive.

Preaching to the Choir

Preaching to the choir—
sometimes it's like being a lonely duck,
knowing that they really do get it,
even though they may appear complacent
with their trite faces puckered up.
I know I've preached this sermon
more than once to each of them, all;
still, only a few seem amused.
Two are disillusioned
and one simply appalled,
but I shall keep on preaching
as long as God continues to help me wing it,
and I'll keep on praying for them
as he continues to help them sing it.

Lonelitude

The lonelitude of solitude
I oft do sit and ponder.
Where longitude meets latitude,
a rock I crawl me under.
My time I bide as I hide
like crustaceans in mollusk shells,
where solitude can best be described
as my heaven or my hell.
Birds that sing in early dawn,
I hear them very well,
but not as clear as the lonely song
sung by the nightingale.

Where Am I in My Life?

Where's the pleasure in this life?
I believe I have lived long enough.
I feel the pain of my past.
Where's the happiness that comes?
When the past never simply just goes away,
where are my better days? I don't have many left.
Stifled in my mind are haunting thoughts.
Is this the party life has brought?
Still the same, I'm getting used to it,
as if fate for me is nothing more
than the roar of discourse.
Yet I refuse to give in,
even though I am so perplexed within.
Is there anything left in life for me
than the common oddity of monotony?

Tucking in the Mannequins

Tucking in the mannequins—
not as easy as one may think.
They masquerade as someone,
no one you have ever seen,
and yet their charade is to be
dressed up and ready to go,
but without me they can't leave again—
something I think they know.
It's time to tuck in the mannequins;
like children, they refuse to go,
but then suddenly they are sleepy,
posed in their finest of clothes,
as if totally confused. None of them
to bed want to go.
With displaying eyes,
they tell their lies,
staring distantly into the night.
But once again it's time again
for tucking in the mannequins.
Time to turn out the light.
So it's off to bed for the mannequins,
and not a first word shall they speak.
They ought to know when it's time for them
to go to bed and sleep.
With a cold, hard glare, a constant stare,
wishing they had some place to be,
I say good night to the mannequins.
Not one says good night to me.

A Friend Now Foe

What fool am I
that I should trust
meaningless words
that settle like dust.
A friend now foe
has woven my woes,
accepting my affection
indiscreetly with deception.
Then comes the wind
stirring again,
carrying away
the dust and the friend.
And all that is left
are the remnant woes
of a pretending friend,
a fawning foe.

Learning to Live Again

Love Like Nothing Else

People will lead you to believe
that there's something else,
but something else is what they have in mind.
When you leave what you have
to find something else,
you may leave the best behind.
But then again, if there's nothing left,
is leaving still a crime?
Love is like nothing else,
and nothing else will you find
if you keep looking for something else
like you left behind.
Keep believing in yourself,
and one day you will find
a love like nothing else,
nothing you had in mind.

My Time Alone

When my heart is empty
and full of despair,
I spend time with him.
My troubles I bare.
Why would he listen?
Why would he care?
I'm such a mess,
even before my brothers.
And when I find myself
constantly falling,
still I hear his voice
of rescue calling.
He refuses to let me slip
from the grip of his hands.
Though I alter my path,
I cannot alter his plan.
Like summer showers,
he covers me in his grace,
washing away a past
no man can erase.
Every time all hope
appears to be gone,
I find him awaiting me
in my time alone.

The Crowded World of Love and Laughter

The crowded world of love and laughter
emerging from the befores and afters,
humilities that often don indebted hapless,
forever seemingly to slowly drift.
In a river of life that rushes too swift,
true friends, new friends—may they all remain,
recurring with grandeur
to disperse life's remnant pains
from many hearts and the paths they've taken,
a meandrous maze of perils forsaken.
Was not, is not, life too much?
And its ransom rancor for many,
such constant torment that's never ending,
but ought the bounty for its capture
be a crowded world of love and laughter?

Runners' Highs and Runners' Lows

Runners' highs and runners' lows
rest on beaches with blistered toes.
They dream of faster times
from all the laps
that they run on the track,
but a runner's race
is the only time
for all their labor.
They have their wine,
and with the training
and what they refuse to eat,
they plan their life
in order to peak—
when to work and when to sleep,
what shoes to wear, and
what friends they keep.
It is a race,
racing now
in their thoughts
as they determine how
to approach the hills
they shall run up and down,
how best to endure
the remaining miles.
The pain is plenty
and injuries many,
but a runner believes

he or she survives all in time.
Like oceans tides
that ebb and flow,
a runner runs
on highs and lows.

Dental Floss

Dental floss rids the things
caught between my teeth.
I wish I had some dental floss
to rid my life
of the things I do not need.

Funny Lessons of Life

The funny lessons we learn in life
aren't always the lessons
that come from pains and strife.
Some are those silly times
when we laugh out loud
after climbing our mountains
and reaching the clouds.
The greatest of lessons
in this life we live
are those we learn
from the people who take
and the people who give.

Whiners and Complainers

There are whiners and complainers,
and some are simply explainers.
But the work usually gets done
by the not-so-worrisome ones.

Dance and Lean as We Grow

What say you, wind whispering so?
Who's the enemy of my soul?
Tales telling when you blow.
In my fable, who's my foe?
When you come,
when you go,
trees dance and lean,
but still they grow,
never questioning friend or foe.
Teach me how to dance and lean
like trees when you blow again,
free from questions that control,
like "Who's my friend and who's my foe?"

Young Runner

She smiles inconspicuously,
knowing more than she leads you to believe.
Still young and unassuming,
she sees the good in everyone she meets.
She ponders not as seasons change
what is lost or what is gained,
always wise indiscriminately
with beauty abounding nondeliberately.
She awaits more than fate to find
true love her heart cannot deny.
But until that time, she resides
to delight in a simpler life,
grinning somewhat innocently
at little things others fail to see.

There's No Time Left

And the daylight sends
a gentle wind
that wrestles through the trees.
A blue jay sings
as a honeybee
hovers over me.
It flies away as I sway
In a hammock where I lie
And the clouds float by
like ice-cream floats,
vanilla in the sky,
and the day's last rays
of sunshine wave
as if to say good-bye.
And wind and time
momentarily unwind.
Taking their final breath
and I, in my hammock,
still have a thousand dreams
for which today
there's no time left.

Endless Night, Endless Sun

Eyes searching the sky at night,
waiting on the stars to fall,
a million dots of light.
No one can count them all.
The morning glow,
rising slow,
and one by one,
the stars must go.
Even the brightest
dims twilight-less
while trees emerge
from tree lines they were

And rooftops of houses
that looked like mountains
separate to each
a new home.
The moon with its shimmer
loses its glimmer
as daylight slowly comes,
and with all its mysteries and myth,
the night comes with.
It chases after the
never-setting
setting sun.

Love

Deep in My Heart

Deep in my heart,
where the sound of its beat
would not permit my head to sleep,
there throbs my love for you
in a musical way,
deep in my heart,
until it ceases to play.

Winter Warms Me

Like the feel of the chill upon my feet
when held together near the warm fire's heat,
winter warms me when I respire
and think of you, my heart's desire.

As if once we have already met,
I imagine the pounding of our hearts
as our bodies together, sweat.
Winter warms me with thoughts of you.
It flows like honey, my body through.

While the snow outside seemingly never melts,
I feel warmth from you I have never felt.
And as each day passes, I find this true:
winter warms me when I think of you.

Struck for You

You are a shadow of my imagination running wild,
a song in my soul that sings to my heart,
Bathed in beauty like sensual art.
Run to me as you are.

You are like a deep-rooted tree
that, though it may sway, withstands the wind,
yet you are beautiful like a setting sun
that paints the sky at each day's end.

Sing to me with your smile and charm.
Come dance with me in my arms.
Live life. Together let's run.

You renew my hope that love is still a seed
waiting to sprout among the willows and reeds.
Upon this lake deep in my heart,
you are a dream of desires that never departs.

Love Should Be Like This

Your eyes light up the sky
from the moment I see them
until they are gone.
Why does the mystery of love
lead us down paths
we'd never venture on
and bring to life
secrets of the heart
our hearts have never known?
Under no control am I.
Each time I think of you,
you simply stir my soul.
I know not what to do,
but maybe love should be like this—
your beautiful smile,
your charming style,
all delightful reminisce,
the dreams I dream
of you and me,
awaiting our first kiss.
And if we are to never be
together as I wish,
I believe with all my heart
still that love should be like this.

Heaven's Dew

A gentle breeze,
an autumn sky,
a soul set free
anywhere to fly—
what says a heart
that wants to speak,
yet knows not if
to itself should keep
whispers of someone new
who awakens it from
its restless sleep?
And to the dreams
that never seize,
which steal away
like a thief,
a heart proclaimed
to be free,
and so a soul free to fly
flies to where the heart decides,
reasoning not with wisdom's words
or sound advice often heard.
Sacred things we hold dear in life
are people we never forget
and love we hope to find.
From her golden skin
to her midnight hair,
she has sung to my soul
with only a stare.

More than a Chance

Sing to my soul. Your whispers I hear,
sweet treasures of the heart dancing in my ears.
Lips that set fire before they are kissed,
yours invite me to a place I cannot resist.
With tangled tongues, I am so lost in you.
Every song is a mystery for a magical dance
to hold you, to be with you.
Love is more than a chance,
more than a whim or an enchanting encounter.
To dance with you is not just a dance,
for when I am with you,
love is more than a chance.

Laurie

The peculiar innocence of one who hides
in between the shadows of an imaginary life—
her life lived within her mind.
She does not see
her uncommon style,
her soul that freely roams
like an exploring child.
Graced with a beauty
like a horse in the wild,
impeccable with an inner strength,
she longs for nothing else
than to be at peace with herself.

Purple Flowers

Purple flowers in a field, forever
dancing with the winds of time,
forever kept like secrets held,
in cellars of best-kept wine.

She approaches life with artistry.
one of beauty and simplicity;
she holds to values she believes,
retreating only to her honesty.

Her smile reveals a devilish innocence,
a twist of happiness, a hidden hope.
She relentlessly pursues nothing.
Like purple flowers in a field, forever
she dances in the winds of time.

Color Me Kisses

Color me gray on a rainy day
when all the trees have lost their leaves.
Sometimes I find I feel that way.
Shadows grow wherever I go,
yet it's me who slowly fades.

Color me blue when I think of you.
You light up the nothings of my sky.
Sing a song, and I will listen,
even when the words you whisper,
not letting one go casually by.

Color me kisses, all from you.
All my wishes are that you do.
Play with my heart and then run away,
but desert it though
you may not may.

She Grows upon My Heart

She grows upon my heart
like leaves of a tree
in a tree without leaves,
covered in the winter's snow
where not even stems
on the limbs now grow.
Yet the leaves unseen
come spring, I know,
shall cover these limbs
now covered in snow.
So many they'll be
shall dance the tree
down to its roots
when then the wind blows.

Imagine Her in Love with Me

She may not know,
but I've told her so.
She steals my heart
wherever I go.
She teases me
when she smiles
and disappears,
like the many miles
I've traveled
when hoping to find
someone like her,
who robs me blind
of every breath,
of air I breathe,
when I imagine her
in love with me.

Believe in Love

When someone comes along
and holds your hand
just for a little while,
and it wraps your heart
like a warm blanket
in the cool morning air,
and you drive for hours,
leaving her behind,
but a part of her goes with you,
and with her a part of you stays.
You believe again in true love
that never goes away.

The Treasure of Love

Treasures you'll search for;
treasures you'll find.
Treasures kept on a shelf
tarnish in time.
But treasures of the heart
are forever new,
and when you give away
the treasure of love,
the treasure of one
becomes the treasure of two.

Afterthoughts

Like shades of gray often found
in the thin layers of broken clouds
where storms have passed
and winds have ceased,
traces of love similarly surround
in subtle quietness of lonely retreat
a heart that was touched
a love that was real,
beauty that still abounds,
like the picturesque of a painted sky
with ribbons of silver linings
that illuminate the end of the day
when the sun breaks through shining.

The Woman Inside

There is a woman who lives inside
the body of her thoughts,
like photos in her mind.
They pass her by one frame at a time.
She longs for something other
than what she has now,
like flowers before the spring,
just seeds in the ground.
She waits on the warmth
that she has not found—
someone to cuddle, someone to hold,
someone who can see
the tears of her soul.
When the night leaves her,
she becomes busy with the chores of her day,
wondering if her heart has deceived her,
but the feelings never go away.

It Only Lasts Awhile

You ever miss someone
you never got to know?
Thought you'd never be
in love like this so?
Wonderful to meet her,
even though
there may never be
a time for you to grow
with the feelings and emotions
between you that flow.
Every time you think of her,
she makes you smile.
Every time you try to forget her,
it only lasts awhile.
And you wish that this time
it would all work out,
even though nothing
has really started somehow.
You ponder if there may be
another girl you just haven't found
as wonderful as the one
you're missing right now,
a girl who caught your eye
with more than her smile.
And every time you try to forget her
it only lasts awhile.

Snowflakes Falling Late in Spring

To my heart, what often clings
are snowflakes falling late in spring.
And fooled are flowers early blooming
and pretty faces unassuming.
Someone steals what has been stolen
yet again with words unspoken.
A robin sits on a limb and sings
while snowflakes fall late in spring.

The Art of You

Your smile, your warmth, your natural way—
brushstrokes of beauty that take my breath away.
You move my soul to places it has never gone,
but then until I met you, my soul had not known
of the tranquil garden that only love can create,
where everything blooms and a heart can escape
to a safe place it desires to be,
endeared to you in total harmony.
That is the art of you—
you reveal the simple truth
that though I can make it on my own,
life is not meant for me to live alone.
The art of you
reveals the heart of me,
and the heart of me
desires you to be a part of me.

Cappuccino

Like frappé or froth,
and even the weather,
one's cold, one's hot,
one's worse, and one's better.
And whom you ask,
those lovers who treasure,
one says sweet,
the other bitter,
like love itself—
often measured.
Cold or hot,
worse or better,
our frappé or froth,
we choose our pleasure.
To be in love or not
is like the weather.

Rio

Love is not a cliff from which you fall,
one you choose to spread your wings,
hoping to fly if you try,
but fearing you'll fail giving it your all.
It begins in the valley,
a jungle of sorts
beside the roaring streams
where life is plentiful,
yet you are lost.
It is the person who walks with you
through the unknown,
trying to find a higher ground.
It is the adventure together
where the unexpected lies in the path.
It is a bridge of trust
built from two sides
that meets in the middle,
trusses of trust forged
in every moment of trouble and triumph.
We hold no less
to the bond of our hearts
that grows along the way.
And one day, we emerge
above the forest floor,
surrounded by only the beauty
of the mountain we've climbed
where two paths joined to become one.

Judge from Outside (Juiz de Fora)

Is not the heart a kind of stone
with pure, washed wales in ocean's foam,
decaying to dust from which it comes?
No, it is a stem that derives
support from climbing ever higher,
creeping to every place it finds
to drape the soul like wisteria vines.
Judge not the heart
for its unending lies,
full of wisdom and never wise,
but see the love
when soaring high.
judge from outside.

In Its Season

What once were flowers
have now become weeds.
What once were fruits
have now become seeds.
What once was love
hath no more leaves.
What once has withered,
for whatever reason,
will grow again
in its season.

She Smiles Silently

She smiles silently
when she smiles at me.
We talk too much
for it to be
casually engaging
conversationally.
And when we say good-bye,
we never leave
the dreams of our possibilities.
She steals my breath
effortlessly,
making my heart
a foaming sea
from the waves that crash,
its every beat
leaving me breathless
when they recede
all from her smile.
She smiles silently.

Touching the Stars

If I could touch each star
on a clear autumn night,
thousands that glow
with twinkles of light,
I'd rather be with you,
savoring the sight,
holding you close,
laughing at life,
for even the stars
can look down and see
it is you in my heart
that shines bright in me.

Daughters

The Love of My Heart

The love of my heart lives
in you each day,
when you run, when you play.
I am always proud of you,
and I pray for you every day.
You bring so much joy to me.
You are the greatest gift from God
I have ever received.
You are the delight of my soul
and the love of my heart.
He created you in his image,
but you look a little like me.
Run strong in this life.
Enjoy each day you live.
You are so beautiful.
You are my true princess,
the love of my heart.

Kelsey

She's beautiful to me.
Our love forever flows.
Her heart is bigger
than any I know.
Whatever she does,
wherever she goes,
my heart is with her
Forever I know.
I'm sad when she leaves,
troubled when she's gone,
always impatient
for her to come home.
I am trying a little harder,
reluctantly letting go.
As she goes away a little longer
and continues to grow,
if we could only smile
when we say good-bye
and not see the tears
that well up in our eyes.
Yet there will always be a peace
from this love we share—
a love that never leaves
but follows us everywhere.

Conversations with My Daughters

Between the pages of my yesterday,
I have bookmarked my favorite passages of life—
conversations with my daughters
when they were just little girls.
Other chapters filled with dreams of mine
have all but vanished
casually in time,
and the caustic ways
found every day
of who's doing wrong
and who's doing right
all but fade into irrelevancies of life.
This growing love
we give and receive
flourishes like the corn cockles,
flowers among weeds.
And the wonderful world
ahead that waits
comes none too soon
and none to late
as together we grow
and together we write,
from conversations with my daughters,
new pages of life.

Another Day

Another day, I never said,
"Let's wait for it to come.
We'll do the simple things we like,
and then we'll have some fun."

Another day, I rocked you
until the morning sun.
You were just a baby who couldn't sleep,
but I was the sleepless one.

Another day we brought your sister home
for the first time for you to hold.
You smiled as if it was Christmas.
It doesn't seem that long ago.

Another day, you were holding my hand,
learning to walk ever so far.
Another day you wrecked your bike
and bent the handlebars.

I was never anxious
for another day to come
because I knew we would be closer
to the day we are now upon.

And now I can only reminisce
of the days when you were young.
You're about to leave for college.
Too quickly another day has come.

To My Daughters

I don't know where your road shall lead,
but I know if you love the way you have loved others,
if you give the way you have unselfishly given,
if your heart remains as pure as it is now,
then the road ahead will bend before you,
and even the stars may follow behind,
and the love you've always managed to share
is the kind this world desperately hopes to find.